Editor in Chief
Ina Massler Levin, M.A.

Editor
Eric Migliaccio

Contributing Editor
Sarah Smith

Creative Director
Karen J. Goldfluss, M.S. Ed.

Cover Design
Tony Carrillo / Marilyn Goldberg

Teacher Created Resources, Inc.

6421 Industry Way
Westminster, CA 92683
www.teachercreated.com

ISBN: 978-1-4206-5926-9

©2008 Teacher Created Resources, Inc.
Reprinted, 2013 (PO6593)
Made in U.S.A.

This book belongs to

_____

Ready·Set·Learn

Get Ready to Learn!

Get ready, get set, and go! Boost your child's learning with this exciting series of books. Geared to help children practice and master many needed skills, the *Ready·Set·Learn* books are bursting with 64 pages of learning fun. Use these books for . . .

- ※ enrichment
- ※ skills reinforcement
- ※ extra practice

With their smaller size, the *Ready·Set·Learn* books fit easily in children's hands, backpacks, and book bags. All your child needs to get started are pencils, crayons, and colored pencils.

A full sheet of colorful stickers is included. Use these stickers for . . .

- ※ decorating pages
- ※ rewarding outstanding effort
- ※ keeping track of completed pages

Celebrate your child's progress by using these stickers on the reward chart located on the inside cover. The blue-ribbon sticker fits perfectly on the certificate on page 64.

With *Ready·Set·Learn* and a little encouragement, your child will be on the fast track to learning fun!

Word Problems #1

Directions: Solve the problems.

---

1. Timmy had 8 green marbles. He gave 6 marbles to his friend Mateo. How many marbles does Timmy have left?

8 – 6 = ___2___

He has ___2___ marbles left.

---

2. Jessie bought 2 stickers. Her father gave her some stickers. Now Jessie has 6 stickers in all. How many stickers did her father give her?

2 + _____ = 6

Her father gave her _____ stickers.

---

3. Uncle Jethro collects hats. He has 9 hats. He gave 7 to his nephew. How many hats does Uncle Jethro have left?

9 – 7 = _____

Uncle Jethro has _____ hats left.

---

4. Daisy has 8 pink bows and 1 yellow bow. How many bows does Daisy have in all?

8 + 1 = _____

She has _____ bows.

---

5. Suzy gathered 2 orange leaves. Then she gathered some brown leaves. She now has 7 leaves in all. How many brown leaves did she gather?

2 + _____ = 7

She gathered _____ brown leaves.

---

6. Brad picked several small flowers. He picked 2 large flowers. He now has 5 flowers. How many small flowers did Brad pick?

_____ + 2 = 5

Brad picked _____ small flowers.

Word Problems #2

Directions: Solve the problems. Show your work.

1. My grandma made 4 fruitcakes. My mother made 5 fruitcakes. How many fruitcakes did they make in all? They made _____ fruitcakes.	**2.** My dad baked 5 hams. My grandpa baked 4 hams. How many hams did they bake in all? They baked _____ hams.
3. I made 8 cookies. My friend Mimi ate 2 cookies. How many cookies do we have left? We have _____ cookies left.	**4.** My mom cooked 7 chickens. My dad cooked 3 chickens. How many chickens did they cook in all? They cooked _____ chickens.
5. Hope picked 7 strawberries. Jim ate 4 of them. How many strawberries does Hope have left? Hope has _____ strawberries left.	**6.** Christie picked 3 lemons and 4 limes. How many lemons and limes does Christie have in all? Christie has _____ lemons and limes.

Word Problems #3

Directions: Solve the word problems. Color the squares with even answers blue. Color the squares with odd answers green.

1. Tim had 6 toy cars. For his birthday, he got 4 more. Now he has _____ toy cars.	**2.** Two gloves have 10 fingers. One glove has _____ fingers.	**3.** Mary had 10 pennies. She lost 2 of them. Mary has _____ pennies left.
4. One tricycle has 3 wheels. Three tricycles have _____ wheels.	**5.** One octopus has 8 legs. Two octopi have _____ legs.	**6.** Billy had 12 blocks. Five were brown. _____ were blue.
7. One week has 7 days. Two weeks have _____ days.	**8.** Jim has 6 gumdrops. Bob gives him 5 more. Jim now has _____ gumdrops.	**9.** Dan and Sue each had 1 dime. Each dime is 10 cents. Together they have _____ cents.

Word Problems #4

Directions: Read each word problem. Write the number sentence it shows. Find the difference.

1. A dog was walking through his yard when he saw 7 cats on the fence. He barked, and 6 cats ran away. How many cats were left?

_____
number sentence

_____
answer

2. A woman grew a vegetable garden, and in it were 8 ears of corn. She picked 2 ears on one day, 0 ears on the next, and 6 ears on the third day. How many ears of corn were left in her garden?

_____
number sentence

_____
answer

3. The monkey had 10 bananas. He ate 1 the first day and 6 the second. How many bananas were left?

_____
number sentence

_____
answer

4. A boy had 5 assignments for homework. He completed 3 before dinner and 1 after dinner. How many assignments were left?

_____
number sentence

_____
answer

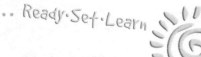

Word Problems #5

Directions: Solve each problem. Show your work.

1. Oscar had 8 cookies. His friend gave him some more cookies. Now Oscar has 11 cookies. How many cookies did Oscar's friend give him?

Oscar's friend gave him _____ cookies.

2. Frances had 9 puzzles. Her dad gave her some more puzzles. Now Frances has 12 puzzles. How many puzzles did Frances's dad give her?

Frances's dad gave her _____ puzzles.

3. Lisa had 12 candy bars. Her brother ate some of them. Now there are only 4 left. How many candy bars did her brother eat?

Her brother ate _____ candy bars.

4. Bart had 10 packs of gum. His sister took several packs of gum. Bart has only 3 packs left. How many packs of gum did his sister take?

His sister took _____ packs of gum.

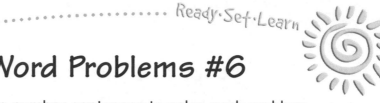

Word Problems #6

Directions: Create number sentences to solve each problem.

1. The elevator can take 10 people. There are 3 people in the elevator right now. How many more can fit into the elevator?

   | 10 | – | 3 | =

   _____ people

2. The parking lot can take 20 cars. If there are 14 cars parked already, how many more cars can park in the parking lot?

   | | – | | =

   _____ cars

3. 12 eggs can fit into the egg carton. If there are 6 eggs in the carton, how many more can be put into the carton?

   | | – | | =

   _____ eggs

4. 5 people can fit into the car. If there are 3 people in the car, how many more can fit?

   | | – | | =

   _____ people

5. 12 pencils fit into a pencil box. If there are 9 pencils in the box, how many more pencils can fit in?

   | | – | | =

   _____ pencils

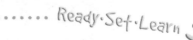

Word Problems #7

Directions: Solve the problems. Show your work.

---

1. Lassie ate 5 dog bones for breakfast and 9 for lunch. How many dog bones did Lassie eat in all?

She ate _____ bones.

2. Benji barked 8 times at the mail carrier and 3 times at the meter reader. How many times did Benji bark?

Benji barked _____ times.

---

3. Max bought 12 pounds of dog food. His dog Heidi ate 6 pounds of it. How many pounds of dog food does Max have left?

Max has _____ pounds left.

4. The dog had 10 fleas. If 2 fleas jumped off, how many fleas were left?

The dog had _____ fleas left.

---

5. Cybill had 11 dogs, but she gave 2 away. How many dogs does Cybill have now?

Cybill has _____ dogs now.

6. Jesse's dog had 14 puppies, but 3 were given to his neighbor. How many puppies does Jesse have left?

Jesse has _____ puppies left.

---

10 ©*Teacher Created Resources, Inc.*

Word Problems #8

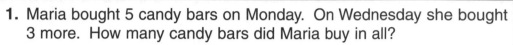

Directions: Circle the letter next to the correct answer.

---

1. Maria bought 5 candy bars on Monday. On Wednesday she bought 3 more. How many candy bars did Maria buy in all?

    A. 2   C. 3

    B. 5   D. 8

---

2. Ron has 5 baseball cards, 7 football cards, and 2 soccer cards. How many sports cards does Ron have in all?

    A. 7   C. 9

    B. 12   D. 14

---

3. Lin and Jose were playing checkers. Lin won 6 games and Jose won 4 games. How many games did they play?

    A. 10   C. 6

    B. 4   D. 12

---

4. At the Springton Zoo Reptile House there are 2 lizards, 4 snakes, and 3 turtles. How many reptiles are there in all?

    A. 7   C. 9

    B. 8   D. 10

---

5. Gus bought 2 tickets to the school play. The tickets cost $4 each. Which number sentence tells how to find out how much money Gus spent altogether?

    A. $1 + $4 = $6   B. $6 − $4 = $2

    C. $4 + $4 = $8   D. $8 − $4 = $4

---

6. In the morning there were 7 crows on the old oak tree. In the afternoon 8 more crows joined them. How many crows in all were in the old oak tree?

    A. 7   B. 15

    C. 8   D. 16

Word Problems #9

Directions: Solve the problems.

1. Jenny made 8 pizzas. Tammy made 6 pizzas. How many pizzas did they make in all?

   They made _____ pizzas.

2. Chester saw 6 clouds that looked like lions and 9 clouds that looked like tigers. How many clouds did Chester see in all?

   Chester saw _____ clouds.

3. I have 13 books from my brother and sister. My sister gave me 7 of the books. How many books did my brother give me?

   My brother gave me _____ books.

4. Dad has 12 kites. If 7 of them are box kites, how many are not box kites?

   _____ are not box kites.

5. There were 9 dandelions in Terri's front yard and 8 in her backyard. How many dandelions were there in all?

   There were _____ dandelions.

6. Dennis earned 14 game points. He needs 18 points to win. How many more points must he earn to win?

   He must earn _____ more points.

Word Problems #10

Directions: Circle the correct number sentences.

1. Joan made 12 tacos. Her son ate 6 of them. How many tacos were left?

   12 – 6 = 6   12 + 6 = 18

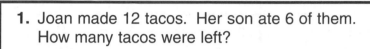

2. Hector ate 11 chips and 5 apple slices. How many things did Hector eat in all?

   11 + 5 = 16   11 – 5 = 6

3. Rachel made 7 tortillas. Her sister made 6 tortillas. How many tortillas were made in all?

   7 – 6 = 1   7 + 6 = 13

4. Hector ordered 10 enchiladas and 8 tacos. How many things did Hector order in all?

   10 + 8 = 18   10 – 8 = 2

5. Hope ate 15 grapes. Grace ate 6 fewer grapes than Hope. How many grapes did Grace eat?

   15 + 6 = 21   15 – 6 = 9

6. Tony's family ate 16 peppers and 3 avocados. How many more peppers did Tony's family eat than avocados?

   16 + 3 = 19   16 – 3 = 13

Word Problems #11

Directions: Solve the problems. Show your work.

---

1. Yolanda had 7 marbles. She won 7 more in the marble tournament. How many marbles does Yolanda now have?

Yolanda now has _____ marbles.

2. Jeff planted 6 tomato seeds and 8 carrot seeds. How many seeds did Jeff plant in all?

Jeff planted _____ seeds.

---

3. Gene had 14 worms. He used 8 of them when he went fishing. How many worms does Gene have left?

Gene has _____ worms left.

4. Roberta caught 12 fish. She set 7 of them free. How many fish does Roberta have left?

Roberta has _____ fish left.

14

Ready·Set·Learn

Word Problems #12

Directions: Solve the problems. Show your work.

---

1. Penny has 2 red rings, 7 green rings, and 1 white ring. How many rings does Penny have in all?

Penny has _____ rings.

2. Christopher has 5 pennies, 2 nickels, and 7 dimes. How many coins does he have in all?

Christopher has _____ coins.

3. There were 13 aphids on Lucas' roses. He brushed 8 of them off. How many aphids were left?

There are _____ aphids left.

4. Jonas planted 18 flowers in his yard. The grasshoppers ate 9 of them. How many flowers does Jonas have left?

Jonas has _____ flowers left.

5. Doug collects flowers. He has 5 roses and 9 wildflowers in his collection. How many flowers does Doug have in all?

Doug has _____ flowers.

6. Trevor saw 13 bushes. If 7 of them had flowers, how many bushes did not have flowers?

_____ bushes did not have flowers.

Word Problems #13

Directions: Solve the problems. Show your work.

---

1. Cory planted 13 carrot seeds. Only 5 sprouted. How many carrot seeds did not sprout?

_____ carrot seeds did not sprout.

2. Raven planted 12 squash seeds and 6 tomato seeds. How many seeds did she plant in all?

Raven planted _____ seeds.

---

3. Mr. Clover picked 16 heads of lettuce. He gave us 9 heads of lettuce. How many heads of lettuce does Mr. Clover have left?

Mr. Clover has _____ heads of lettuce left.

4. Mrs. Peabody picked 15 ears of corn. If 6 of the ears had bugs, how many ears did not have bugs?

_____ ears of corn did not have bugs.

---

5. Cecil had 14 butterflies. If 8 of them flew away, how many butterflies does Cecil have left?

Cecil has _____ butterflies left.

6. Kenya found 10 snails in her garden. She picked up 5 of them. How many snails are left in Kenya's garden?

Kenya has _____ snails left in her garden.

Word Problems #14

Directions: Solve the problems. Show your work.

---

1. Ms. Smith put 15 vegetables into her pot of soup. If 7 of the vegetables are onions, how many were not onions?

_____ were not onions.

2. Mr. Wimple planted 18 radish seeds. The birds ate 8 of the seeds. How many radish seeds are left?

There are _____ radish seeds left.

---

3. A group of Girl Scouts went camping. If 13 of the girls set up camp while the other 5 went on a hike, how many Girl Scouts were there in all?

There were _____ Girl Scouts.

4. Eight Boy Scouts cooked dinner. The rest set up the tents. There were 14 Boy Scouts in all. How many set up the tents?

_____ Boy Scouts set up the tents.

---

5. Liz bought 7 cat toys and 9 dog toys. How many animal toys did Liz buy in all?

Liz bought _____ animal toys.

6. Ana has 8 yellow fish and 7 silver fish. How many fish does Ana have in all?

Ana has _____ fish.

Word Problems #15

Directions: Read each problem and write the answer in the box. Show your work.

---

1. Kate had $5. If she was given $9 more, how much money does she have?

---

2. If George had 30 marbles and lost 17 marbles, how many does he now have?

---

3. A piece of string is 20 cm long and Ty cuts off 11 cm. How many centimeters of string does Ty have left over?

---

4. In Lamia's garden there are 43 daffodils and 23 pansies. How many flowers are there in Lamia's garden?

18

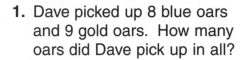

Word Problems #16

Directions: Solve the problems.

1. Dave picked up 8 blue oars and 9 gold oars. How many oars did Dave pick up in all?

   Dave picked up _____ oars.

2. Hilda gathered 6 small twigs and 9 large twigs to build a campfire. How many twigs in all did Hilda gather?

   Hilda gathered _____ twigs.

3. Some members of the Blue Troop were painting rocks. If 2 of the 18 members were painting rocks, how many members were not painting rocks?

   _____ were not painting rocks.

4. Nine of the Red Troop members were making belts. Five of the Orange Troop members were making belts, too. How many members were making belts?

   _____ were making belts.

5. Mrs. Jones had 9 troops on her hike. She picked up 7 more troops along the way. How many troops does she now have?

   She has _____ troops now.

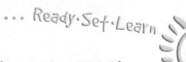

Word Problems #17

Directions: Solve the problems. Show your work.

---

1. The scouts were roasting marshmallows. They burned 3 of the 18 marshmallows. How many marshmallows did not burn?

   _____ marshmallows did not burn.

2. At the crafts station, 6 scouts made bracelets and 8 made hats. How many crafts were made in all?

   There were _____ crafts made.

---

3. The scouts spotted 5 bears and 9 cougars. How many animals did they see?

   The scouts saw _____ animals.

4. One of the scouts sold 7 boxes of cookies on Monday and 6 boxes of cookies on Tuesday. How many boxes did she sell in all?

   She sold _____ boxes.

---

5. Alvin found 16 cardboard boxes. He flattened 8 of them. How many boxes were not flattened?

   _____ boxes were not flattened.

6. Jamal had 15 spoons at the cooking station. If 3 of them fell off the table, how many are left on the table?

   There are _____ spoons left.

Word Problems #18

Directions: Solve the problems. Show your work.

---

1. If I had 7 flowers and bought 8 more, how many would I have altogether?

_____ flowers

---

2. Kylie had 3 cats. She found 9 more. How many cats does Kylie have now?

_____ cats

---

3. There were 17 chocolates but 12 were eaten. How many were left?

_____ chocolates

---

4. Twelve eggs take away no eggs leaves how many eggs?

_____ eggs

---

5. Karen bought 9 cakes and Jason bought 7. How many cakes altogether?

_____ cakes

---

6. Kirsten had 11 marbles, Lachlan had 6 marbles, and Robin had 0 marbles. How many marbles were there altogether?

_____ marbles

---

7. There were 20 fireworks. 12 were used. How many were still left?

_____ fireworks

---

8. Rita saw 8 movies last month. Pam saw 6. How many movies did the two girls see altogether?

_____ movies

Word Problems #19

Directions: Read each word problem. In the box, write the number sentence it shows. Find the sum.

1. Kevin went for a walk and saw 1 frog, 3 cats, and 5 flowers. How many things did he see in all?

_____ + _____ + _____ = _____

2. When Sally got on the school bus, there were 8 boys, 10 girls, and the bus driver already there. How many people were already on the bus?

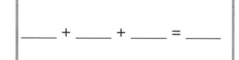

_____ + _____ + _____ = _____

3. John ate a pizza with 7 mushrooms, 7 olives, and 5 pieces of pepperoni. How many pieces of topping were on his pizza in all?

_____ + _____ + _____ = _____

4. Today Joe saw 3 cats, 2 dogs, and 5 puppies in the park. How many animals did he see in all?

_____ + _____ + _____ = _____

Word Problems #20

Directions: Solve the problems. Show your work.

1. Jacob has 5 books. Bart has 3 books. Amy has 2 books. How many books do they have in all? They have _____ books.	**2.** The recipe calls for 1 cup of flour, 5 cups of sugar, and 1 cup of milk. How many cups of ingredients do I need to use? I need to use _____ cups of ingredients.
3. Brittany collected 6 ladybugs, 2 grasshoppers, and 3 butterflies. How many insects did Brittany collect in all? Brittany collected _____ insects.	**4.** There were 8 crows, 1 bluebird, and 1 robin sitting in a tree. How many birds were there in all? There were _____ birds.
5. Rosita had 5 yellow pencils, 1 pink pencil, and 2 green pencils. How many pencils did she have in all? Rosita had _____ pencils.	**6.** Luke had 4 baseball gloves, 5 bats, and 4 baseballs. How many pieces of baseball equipment did Luke have in all? Luke had _____ pieces.

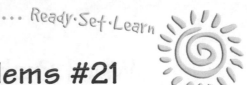

Word Problems #21

Directions: Solve the problems. Show your work.

---

1. Tina has 21 green stamps, 32 red stamps, and 40 blue stamps. How many stamps does Tina have in all?

   Tina has _____ stamps.

2. Ron has 14 yellow cards, 30 purple cards, and 35 black cards. How many cards does Ron have in all?

   Ron has _____ cards.

3. Larry had 8 baseball cards. His dad gave him 3 more. Larry gave his sister 5. How many baseball cards does Larry have left?

   Larry has _____ baseball cards left.

4. Andy had 12 bowling balls. He bought 4 more and sold 9. How many bowling balls does Andy have left?

   Andy has _____ bowling balls left.

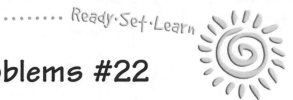

Word Problems #22

Directions: Solve the problems.

---

1. The elephant ate 50 large peanuts and 40 small peanuts. How many peanuts did the elephant eat in all?

$$\begin{array}{r} 50 \\ + 40 \\ \hline \end{array}$$

The elephant ate _____ peanuts.

2. At the morning show, the lion jumped 70 times. During the evening show, the lion jumped 25 times. How many times did the lion jump in all?

$$\begin{array}{r} 70 \\ + 25 \\ \hline \end{array}$$

The lion jumped _____ times.

---

3. There were 95 fleas in the flea circus. 60 fleas jumped away. How many fleas were left in the circus.

$$\begin{array}{r} 95 \\ - 60 \\ \hline \end{array}$$

_____ fleas were left in the flea circus.

4. The monkeys ate 35 bananas in the morning and 20 bananas in the evening. How many bananas did the monkeys eat in all?

$$\begin{array}{r} 35 \\ + 20 \\ \hline \end{array}$$

The monkeys ate _____ bananas.

---

5. The tiger has 85 stripes. The zebra has 30 fewer stripes than the tiger. How many stripes does the zebra have?

$$\begin{array}{r} 85 \\ - 30 \\ \hline \end{array}$$

The zebra has _____ stripes.

6. The seal ate 85 pounds of fish on Monday and 55 fewer pounds of fish on Tuesday. How many pounds of fish did the seal eat on Tuesday?

$$\begin{array}{r} 85 \\ - 55 \\ \hline \end{array}$$

The seal ate _____ pounds of fish on Tuesday.

Word Problems #23

Directions: Solve the problems. Show your work.

---

1. Zipporah saw 15 paw prints. Lacey saw 13 fewer paw prints than Zipporah. How many paw prints did Lacey see?

   Lacey saw _____ paw prints.

2. Misty saw 43 turtles. Mabel saw 10 fewer turtles than Misty. How many turtles did Mabel see?

   Mabel saw _____ turtles.

---

3. Isaac has 22 peanuts. Pam has 17 more peanuts than Isaac. How many peanuts does Pam have?

   Pam has _____ peanuts.

4. Patty has 32 headbands. Cathy has 22 fewer headbands than Patty. How many headbands does Cathy have?

   Cathy has _____ headbands.

---

5. Candace went on the camel ride 41 times. Patrice went on the camel ride 18 times. How many times did the girls ride the camel in all?

   The girls rode the camel _____ times.

6. Sean fed the monkey 31 peanuts. Thomas fed the monkey 24 peanuts. How many peanuts did the monkey eat?

   The monkey ate _____ peanuts.

26

Word Problems #24

Directions: Solve each problem.

1. Angelo has 57 turtles and 22 iguanas. How many pets does Angelo have in all? Angelo has _____ pets.	2. Kate has 29 baseballs and 50 hockey pucks. How many pieces of equipment does Kate have in all? Kate has _____ pieces of equipment.

Directions: Read each problem. Circle the **+** or **−** sign to show which one you would use to solve the problem.

3. Janice has 49 hair bows. She gives 25 of them to her cousin. How many hair bows does Janice have left? **+** **−**	4. Sully has 25 pencils. He buys 41 more. How many pencils does Sully now have? **+** **−**
5. Elora has 83 aluminum cans. She collects 14 more. How many cans does Elora now have? **+** **−**	6. Max has 22 pieces of gum. He gives 6 pieces to his best friend, Leonard. How many pieces does Max now have? **+** **−**

Word Problems #25

Directions: Solve the problems. Show your work.

1. There were 64 jellybeans in the jar. Now there are only 22 jellybeans. How many jellybeans are missing? There are _____ jellybeans missing.	**2.** Mary Kaye invited 99 people to the party. Only 30 came. How many people did not come to the party? _____ people did not come to the party.
3. Jeremy counted 96 stars on Monday and only 26 on Tuesday. How many fewer stars did Jeremy see on Tuesday than on Monday? Jeremy saw _____ fewer stars on Tuesday.	**4.** Leo baked 30 cupcakes for his class. His dog ate 20 of the cupcakes. How many cupcakes does Leo have left? Leo has _____ cupcakes left.
5. Hansel has 75 pieces of candy. He gives 35 pieces to Gretel. How many pieces of candy does Hansel have left? Hansel has _____ pieces of candy left.	**6.** Ivan recycled 14 cans and 25 bottles. How many items did Ivan recycle in all? Ivan recycled _____ items.

Word Problems #26

Directions: Solve the problems. Show your work.

---

1. Cherry collected 86 cans. She recycled 54 of them. How many cans does Cherry have left?

Cherry has _____ cans left.

---

2. Frank picked up 93 shells. 61 of them were sand dollars. The rest were clam shells. How many clam shells did Frank pick up?

Frank picked up _____ clam shells.

---

3. Jeremy had 400 balloons. 100 of them popped. How many balloons does Jeremy have left?

Jeremy has _____ balloons left.

---

4. Philomena had 700 jellybeans. She sold 300 of them. How many jellybeans does Philomena have left?

Philomena has _____ jellybeans left.

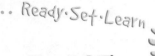

Word Problems #27

Directions: Solve the problems. Show your work.

---

1. Warren had 400 pieces of paper. He put 200 in a notebook. How many pieces of paper are left?

There are _____ pieces of paper left.

2. Nancy colored a pattern using 600 squares. 300 of the squares were red. The rest were blue. How many blue squares were in the pattern?

There were _____ blue squares.

---

3. Scarlett has 220 gumballs and 137 jawbreakers. How many candies does Scarlett have in all?

Scarlett has _____ candies in all.

4. Leroy has 310 bug stickers and 325 sports stickers. How many stickers does Leroy have in all?

Leroy has _____ stickers in all.

Ready·Set·Learn

Word Problems #28

Directions: Read each word problem. In the boxes below each problem, write the number sentence it shows. Find the sum.

1. At the zoo, Kenny saw 4 monkeys, 3 lions, and 4 elephants. How many animals did he see in all?

2. When Sandra went to the tide pools, she counted 12 starfish, 8 crabs, and 16 shells. How many things did she see in all?

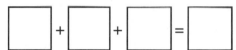

3. During one month, Jared ate 21 sandwiches, 13 apples, and 26 cookies. How many things did he eat in all?

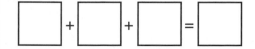

4. Emily did 19 addition problems, 5 multiplication problems, and 31 subtraction problems at school. How many problems did she solve in all?

Word Problems #29

Directions: Read each word problem. Write the number sentence it shows. Find the difference.

---

1. Farmer Cole grew 93 bushels of wheat. Farmer Dale raised 68 bushels. What is the difference in the number of bushels each raised?

$$\boxed{} - \boxed{} = \boxed{}$$

2. Dennis scored 43 points in the basketball game. Claire scored 27. What is the difference between the number of points each scored?

$$\boxed{} - \boxed{} = \boxed{}$$

---

3. Jason bought a pair of shoes for $53. Clark bought a pair for $28. What is the difference paid?

$$\boxed{} - \boxed{} = \boxed{}$$

4. Ted earned $93 working at his mom's office. Paul earned $45 mowing lawns. How much more did Ted earn?

$$\boxed{} - \boxed{} = \boxed{}$$

Word Problems #30

Directions: Solve the problems. Show your work.

1. At the pool there were 46 boys and 38 girls. How many children were at the pool?

2. There were 56 cows and horses in the field. If 27 were horses, how many cows were there?

3. Next month, 67 children will turn 8 years old and 23 children will turn 7 years old. How many children will have birthdays next month altogether?

4. At recess, 28 donuts and 16 muffins were bought. How many donuts and muffins were bought altogether?

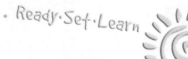

Word Problems #31

Directions: Solve the problems. Show your work.

---

1. Derek had 61 balloons. If 19 of the balloons popped, how many balloons does Derek have left?

Derek has _____ balloons left.

---

2. My sister Cheryl is 35 years old. I am 16 years old. How many years older is Cheryl?

Cheryl is _____ years older.

---

3. Jerry unpacked the light bulbs. There were 67. If 19 were broken, how many light bulbs were not broken?

There were _____ light bulbs not broken.

---

4. Lupe needs 41 candles. There are only 23 candles. How many more does Lupe need?

Lupe needs _____ more candles.

---

5. Eddie has 72 purple rings and 19 green rings. How many rings does Eddie have in all?

Eddie has _____ rings.

---

6. Ariel once caught 38 insects in a net and 64 insects in a box. How many insects did Ariel catch in all?

Ariel caught _____ insects.

34

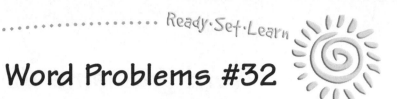

Word Problems #32

Directions: Answer each question below about tadpoles and frogs.

1. 34 eggs in the pond + 15 more eggs were laid How many in all? _____	**2.** 78 eggs under a leaf − 53 eggs hatched How many eggs were left? _____
3. 41 tadpoles swam downstream + 26 tadpoles joined them How many tadpoles altogether? _____	**4.** 99 tadpoles swam in the pond − 62 frogs swam in the pond How many more tadpoles than frogs swam in the pond? _____
5. 87 tree frogs on a tree − 11 snakes each ate a tree frog How many tree frogs are left? _____	**6.** 64 toads were croaking in the pond + 24 toads joined the fun How many toads were croaking in the pond? _____

Word Problems #33

Directions: Solve the problems. Show your work.

---

1. My cousin has 63 coins in his piggy bank. I have 21 coins in my piggy bank. How many coins do we have in all?

   We have _____ coins.

2. Becky is 23 years old. Her dad is 48 years old. If you added their ages together, how old would they be?

   They would be _____ years old.

---

3. When I was cleaning my room, I found 36 socks. I took 14 of them to the laundry room. How many socks do I still have in my room?

   I still have _____ socks in my room.

4. There were 71 birds in the bird show. Angelica saw only 46 of the birds. How many birds did Angelica not see?

   Angelica did not see _____ birds.

---

5. The students made 55 blueberry pancakes and 41 buttermilk pancakes. How many pancakes did they make in all?

   They made _____ pancakes.

6. The zookeeper had 86 crickets in a jar. She gave the tortoise 57 of the crickets. How many crickets does the zookeeper have left?

   The zookeeper has _____ crickets left.

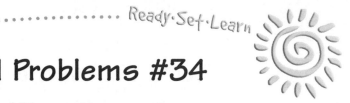

Word Problems #34

Directions: Solve each addition problem.

---

1. Cassidy has 123 pennies. Her friend Todd has 112 pennies. How many pennies do they have together?

   _____ + _____ = _____

---

2. Ken has 312 trading cards. On his birthday, his parents gave him 200 more. How many trading cards does Ken have now?

   _____ + _____ = _____

---

3. Last summer, Ruth and Ruby planted 112 flowers. This summer their friends Pat and Ann helped them plant 100 more. How many flowers did they plant altogether?

   _____ + _____ = _____

---

4. Bobby owns 134 toy cars. Bobby's friend Carl owns 234 toy cars. How many toy cars do the two friends own altogether?

   _____ + _____ = _____

---

5. The local zoo is home to 97 reptiles and 154 mammals. How many total animals live in the zoo?

   _____ + _____ = _____

Word Problems #35

Directions: For each problem, circle the letter next to the correct answer.

1. Robin bought two bags of oranges. Altogether she has 139 oranges. Her family ate 12 oranges. How do you write the number of oranges she has left?

   A. one hundred thirty-nine
   B. one hundred twenty

   C. one hundred seven
   D. one hundred twenty-seven

2. Sandra grilled 24 hamburgers for her family. There were 8 hamburgers left. How many hamburgers did Sandra's family eat?

   A. 24 hamburgers
   B. 8 hamburgers

   C. 16 hamburgers
   D. 32 hamburgers

3. There are 98 seats on an airplane but only 56 passengers. How do you write the number of seats that are empty?

   A. thirty-eight
   B. forty-two

   C. one hundred fifty-four
   D. one hundred forty-four

4. Mrs. Brown made 38 cupcakes. She gave 19 cupcakes to students. What operation should you use to find how many cupcakes were left?

   A. 38 + 19 =
   B. 19 − 38 =

   C. 19 + 38 =
   D. 38 − 19 =

Word Problems #36

Directions: Read the numbers on the jerseys and use them to solve the word problems.

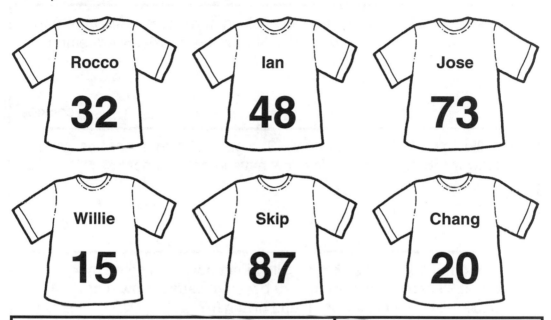

1. Write a number sentence that tells how much more Skip's number is than Jose's.	
2. What is the total of Willie's, Chang's, and Rocco's numbers? Write a number sentence that solves this problem.	
3. Find the total of the largest number and the smallest number on the jerseys. Show this in a number sentence.	
4. Write a number sentence that tells how much more the largest number is than the smallest number.	

Word Problems #37

Directions: Solve these problems and write your answers on the lines.

---

1. Jake put out 38 chocolate chip cookies at his party. After the party, there were only 12 cookies left. How many cookies were eaten at the party?

_____ cookies

---

2. Calley has 35 fish in her bowl. She gave 16 fish to her best friend. How many fish does Calley now have in her fish bowl?

_____ fish

---

3. Jerry had 18 baseball cards. His friend gave him some more baseball cards. He now has 29 baseball cards. How many baseball cards did Jerry's friend give him?

_____ baseball cards

---

4. Jack and Ryan played basketball. Jack scored 32 points and Ryan scored 8 points. How many more points did Jack score than Ryan?

_____ more points

---

5. Antonio and Phil are on the same baseball team. Antonio scored 47 runs this season and Phil scored 28. How many more runs did Antonio score than Phil?

_____ more runs

40

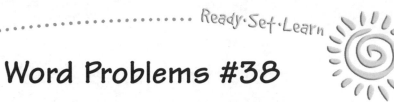

Word Problems #38

Directions: Solve each problem. Draw pictures to show your work.

---

1. Phil had 4 sets of cards. There were 2 cards in each set. How many cards in all?

Phil had _____ cards.

---

2. For her trip to California, Lisa packed 4 shirts and 3 pants. How many shirts and pants did she pack in all?

Lisa packed _____ shirts and pants.

---

3. Sela has 7 boxes of ladybugs. Each box has 3 ladybugs in it. How many ladybugs does Sela have in all?

Sela has _____ ladybugs.

---

4. Kenny has 4 fish hooks. Each hook has 3 worms on it. How many worms are there in all?

There are _____ worms.

Word Problems #39

Directions: Solve each problem.

---

1. Mary cooked 2 meals for her friend each day for 3 days. How many meals did she cook in all? (Write your answer in each box.)

   2 x 3 = ☐

   2 + 2 + 2 = ☐

---

2. Mickey played baseball for 4 days. Each day, he hit 2 home runs. How many home runs did he hit altogether? (Write your answer in each box.)

   4 x 2 = ☐

   2 + 2 + 2 + 2 = ☐

---

3. Shree collects bells. She has 6 bells on each of her 4 shelves. What is the total number of bells Shree has? (Write your answer in each box.)

   6 x 4 = ☐

   6 + 6 + 6 + 6 = ☐

---

4. Seth has 12 mice. He wants to place an equal amount of mice in each of 3 cages. How many mice will go in each cage? (Circle the correct letter.)

   A. 3

   B. 4

   C. 12

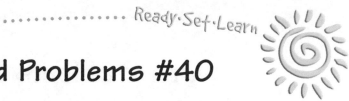

Word Problems #40

Directions: Use multiplication to solve each word problem.

1. Layla played 3 rounds and won 2 marbles in each round. 3 x 2 = _____ Layla won _____ marbles.	**2.** Mel played 2 rounds and won 4 marbles in each round. 2 x 4 = _____ Mel won _____ marbles.
3. Cassie played 5 rounds and won 2 marbles in each round. 5 x 2 = _____ Cassie won _____ marbles.	**4.** Mohammed played 1 round and won 6 marbles. 1 x 6 = _____ Mohammed won _____ marbles.
5. Flavia played 6 rounds and won 2 marbles in each round. 6 x 2 = _____ Flavia won _____ marbles.	**6.** Isidore played 2 rounds and won 7 marbles in each round. 2 x 7 = _____ Isidore won _____ marbles.

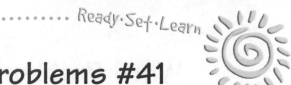

Word Problems #41

Directions: Read each word problem. Write the number sentence you would use to solve each one.

---

1. Crede has two dogs, Kahntu and Princess. Each dog has one dog collar. How many collars are there in all?

   _____ x _____ = _____

---

2. Tommy, Bobby, and James all want to ride the bumper cars. Each person needs three tickets to ride the cars. How many tickets in all do they need?

   _____ x _____ = _____

---

3. There are five giant spiders spinning their webs. Each giant spider has eight giant legs. How many spider legs are there in all?

   _____ x _____ = _____

---

4. Kristen, Allison, Shea, and Derek all had cookies for their snack. Each person ate four cookies. How many cookies were eaten in all?

   _____ x _____ = _____

---

5. Five of the teachers in our school have pet cats. Each one has 3 pet cats. How many pet cats are there in all?

   _____ x _____ = _____

44

Word Problems #42

Directions: Use multiplication to solve each problem. Show your work.

1. Sebastian has 10 hats in 2 boxes. How many hats are there in all? There are _____ hats.	**2.** Eartha has 4 purses. Eartha has 3 coins in each purse. How many coins are there in all? There are _____ coins.
3. Santos has 5 flowers. Each flower has 2 buds. How many buds are there in all? There are _____ buds.	**4.** Maria had 3 books in 3 stacks. How many books are there in all? There are _____ books.
5. Tucker has 2 wheels on 4 bikes. How many wheels are there altogether? There are _____ wheels.	**6.** Gertie has 2 boxes. In each box there are 6 toys. How many toys are there in all? There are _____ toys.

Word Problems #43

Directions: Solve each multiplication problem. Circle the letter next to the correct answer.

1. Mr. Wilson gave 2 candy bars each to Franklin, Pham, and Jose. How many candy bars did he give them in all?

Franklin   Pham   Jose

A. 2   B. 3

C. 6   D. 12

2. Ms. Anderson, the school secretary, sharpened some new pencils. She put 4 pencils into each of 3 containers. Which picture shows the right number of pencils and containers?

A.   B.

C.   D.

3. It takes 4 cups of punch to fill a pitcher. Betsy wants to fill 3 pitchers with punch. How many cups of punch will she need?

    =

A. 4 cups   B. 10 cups

C. 8 cups   D. 12 cups

4. Lupe and Kelly each decorated 6 eggs. They want to display them together. Which container will hold all of their eggs?

A.   B.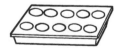

C.   D.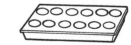

Word Problems #44

Directions: Solve the problems.

---

1. Sari spent 29¢ on gum and 30¢ on candy. How much money did she spend in all?

Sari spent _____¢.

---

2. Rob had 25¢. He earned 10¢ more by raking leaves. How much money does Rob have?

Rob has _____¢.

---

3. Ray had 45¢. He spent 15¢ on a toy. How much money does Ray have left?

Ray has _____¢ left.

---

4. Deb had 95¢. She spent 85¢ on a toy for her cat. How much money does Deb have left?

Deb has _____ ¢ left.

---

5. Bob had 35¢ in his pocket. He put 20¢ into his savings account. How much money does Bob have left in his pocket?

Bob has _____¢ left.

---

6. Sid had 90¢. He gave 60¢ to his brother. How much money does Sid have left?

Sid has _____ ¢ left.

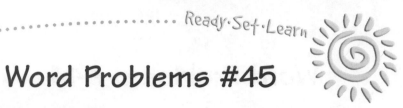

Word Problems #45

Directions: Solve the problems.

---

1. John has 3 dimes. How much money does he have? Does he have enough to by a 25¢ candy bar?

   John has _____ ¢.

   Yes   **No**

2. Franklin has a quarter, a dime, and a penny. How much money does he have in all? Does he have enough to buy a 50¢ cookie?

   Franklin has _____ ¢.

   Yes   **No**

---

3. I have one quarter. How many nickels does it take to make one quarter?

   It takes _____ nickels to make one quarter.

4. I have one quarter. How many pennies does it take to make one quarter?

   It takes _____ pennies to make one quarter.

---

5. Joe had 34¢ in his pocket. If 21¢ fell out the hole in his pocket, how much money does he have left?

   Joe has _____ ¢ left.

6. Esmerelda had 95¢ in her lunch bag. She gave her friend 14¢. How much money does she have left in her lunch bag?

   Esmerelda has _____ ¢.

Word Problems #46

Directions: Solve the problems. Show your work.

1. Helen earned 75¢ washing the car. She put 50¢ in her bank. How much money does Helen have left? Helen has _____¢ left.	**2.** Val's grandma gave her 95¢. Val spent 50¢ on a book. How much money does she have left? Val has _____¢ left.
3. Christine cleaned the pool for 85¢. She bought a pool toy for 73¢. How much money does Christine have left? Christine has _____¢ left.	**4.** Mom had 85¢ in her wallet. She spent 50¢ on a carton of juice. How much money does she have left? Mom has _____¢ left.
5. Mia spent 55¢ on popcorn and 20¢ for gum. How much money did Mia spend in all? Mia spent _____¢.	**6.** Elvis bought an eraser for 45¢ and a pencil for 20¢. How much money did Elvis spend in all? Elvis spent _____¢.

Word Problems #47

Directions: Write each subtraction problem and solve. Use the pictures and prices in the box to help you.

| $42.16 | $51.37 | $10.48 | $30.66 | $24.79 | $11.06 |

1. Rosa has $52.20. She buys a rug. How much money does she have left?

Rosa has _____ left.

$52.20

− $42.16

_____

2. Theo has $79.50. He buys a sofa. How much money does he have left?

Theo has _____ left.

$ __ __ . __ __

− $ __ __ . __ __

_____

$ __ __ . __ __

3. Thomas has $11.75. He buys a new lamp. How much money does Thomas have left?

Thomas has _____ left.

$ __ __ . __ __

− $ __ __ . __ __

_____

$ __ __ . __ __

4. Maurine has $38.95. She buys a new TV set. How much money does Maurine have left?

Maurine has _____ left.

$ __ __ . __ __

− $ __ __ . __ __

_____

$ __ __ . __ __

5. Monty has $86.93. He buys a new table. How much money does Monty have left?

Monty has _____ left.

$ __ __ . __ __

− $ __ __ . __ __

_____

$ __ __ . __ __

Word Problems #48

Directions: Solve each problem.

1. There are 10 napkins in a package and there are 25 students in our class. Each student needs one napkin. Which sentence shows how to find whether there are enough napkins? (*Circle the correct letter.*)

   A. 10 − _____ = 25

   B. 10 + 25 = _____

   C. 25 − 10 = _____

2. For each chocolate cake Sarah bakes, she also bakes three strawberry cakes. If Sarah bakes five chocolate cakes, how many strawberry cakes will she bake? (*Fill in the box.*)

Chocolate Cakes	1	2	3	4	5
Strawberry Cakes	3	6	9	12	

3. There are 35 passengers on a plane. Five passengers can sit in each row. How many rows of seats are needed on the plane? (*Write the math problem on the line. Then solve.*)

   _____

4. Mike drove 198 miles. The next day, he drove 89 miles. How many miles did he drive in all? (*Circle the correct letter.*)

   A. 109

   B. 207

   C. 287

Word Problems #49

Directions: Solve the problems.

1. The play began at 6:00 and lasted 45 minutes. What time did the play end?

   Show it on the clock.

2. Lee's family went on a picnic. They left at 11:00 A.M. and arrived 30 minutes later. What time did they get there?

   Show it on the clock.

3. Luke starts his homework one hour after dinner. If he finishes dinner at 6:30 P.M., when does he start doing his homework?

   Circle the answer.

   5:30 P.M.   **7:30 P.M.**

4. Rachel eats lunch every day at noon. When does Rachel eat lunch?

   Circle the answer.

   11:00 A.M.   **12:00 P.M.**

5. Susan comes home from school at 4:00 P.M. If she eats dinner two hours later, when does Susan eat dinner?

   Write the time.

   _____ : _____ P.M.

6. Sandy went to the school dance at 7:30 P.M. She arrived home 3 hours later. What time did Sandy get home?

   Write the time.

   _____ : _____ P.M.

Word Problems #50

Directions: Circle the correct answer.

---

1. It takes Shirley half an hour to walk to school. She left home at 8:00. What time did she arrive at school?

half past 8

a quarter till 8

2. Jason started warming up for practice at 3:30. He spent 15 minutes warming up. What time did Jason finish?

half past 3

a quarter till 4

---

3. Samantha spent 15 minutes raking leaves. She finished at 5:45. What time did Samantha start raking the leaves?

half past 5

a quarter till 6

4. It took Brent half an hour to wax the car. He finished at 2:45. What time did Brent start waxing the car?

half past 2

a quarter past 2

---

5. Shalom started cleaning her room at 7:00. She finished 15 minutes later. What time did Shalom finish cleaning her room?

a quarter till 7

a quarter past 7

6. Roberto began cooking dinner at 4:15. It took him half an hour to finish cooking. What time was dinner on the table?

half past 4

a quarter till 5

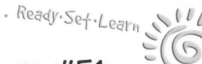

Word Problems #51

Directions: Solve the problems. Show your work.

---

1. I bought a whole pie that had 6 slices. I served half to my friends. How many slices do I have left?

   I have _____ slices of pie.

2. Rocky ordered a pizza. The pizza was cut into 4 equal pieces. Rocky ate half of the pizza. How many pieces did Rocky eat?

   Rocky ate _____ pieces of pizza.

3. Ricky had 9 marbles. He kept 1/3. He gave 1/3 to Sonya and 1/3 to Len. How many marbles does each person now have?

   Each person has _____ marbles.

4. Marilyn had 5 houses. She sold 1/5 of them. How many houses did she keep?

   Marilyn kept _____ houses.

　　　54

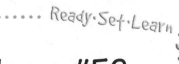

Word Problems #52

Directions: Use the number line to help find the answer.

1. Marybeth counted 9 goats. Annie counted 4 more goats than Marybeth. How many goats did Annie count in all?

Annie counted _____ goats in all.

2. Gordon counted 11 red cows and 4 brown cows. How many cows did Gordon count in all?

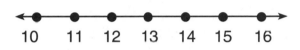

Gordon counted _____ cows in all.

3. Amos counted 10 ewes and 6 lambs. How many sheep did Amos count in all?

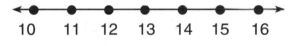

Amos counted _____ sheep in all.

4. Sheila had 15 pigs. She sold 4 of them at the state fair. How many pigs does Sheila have left?

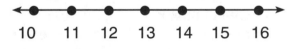

Sheila has _____ pigs left.

5. Rob had 17 ponies. 3 of the ponies were brown. The rest were black. How many black ponies did Rob have?

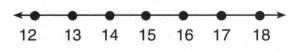

Rob had _____ black ponies.

Word Problems #53

Directions: Fill in the correct answer circle for each problem.

1. Richard is thinking of a number. The number has a 9 in the ones place and a 4 in the hundreds place. What is Richard's number?

934	349	409
◯	◯	◯

2. Maggie is thinking of a number. The number has an 8 in the tens place and an 8 in the hundreds place. What is Maggie's number?

883	838	388
◯	◯	◯

3. Jack is thinking of a number. The number has a 9 in the tens place and a 1 in the ones place. What is Jack's number?

219	291	912
◯	◯	◯

4. Celia is thinking of a number. The number has a 5 in the hundreds place and a 4 in the tens place. What is Celia's number?

745	457	547
◯	◯	◯

5. Alec is thinking of a number. The number has a 2 in the tens place and a 2 in the ones place. What is Alec's number?

262	622	226
◯	◯	◯

Word Problems #54

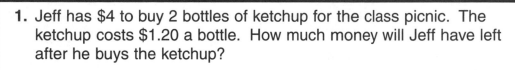

Directions: Circle the letter next to the correct answer.

---

1. Jeff has $4 to buy 2 bottles of ketchup for the class picnic. The ketchup costs $1.20 a bottle. How much money will Jeff have left after he buys the ketchup?

   A. $1.20   B. $1.60

   C. $2.40   D. $2.60

---

2. Della has 22 sports cards. She has 7 baseball cards and 8 football cards. The rest of the cards are soccer cards. How many soccer cards does Della have?

   A. 7   B. 14

   C. 8   D. 15

---

3. Chan made 17 origami frogs. He gave 5 to Lin and 3 to Maria. How many frogs did Chan have left?

   A. 3   B. 8

   C. 5   D. 9

---

4. Gary's allowance is $5 a week, and Shamika's is $4 a week. Over a period of 4 weeks, how much more money does Gary receive?

   A. $5   B. $4

   C. $3   D. $2

---

5. Marilyn and her family went on a vacation for 14 days. They spent 5 days in Germany and 4 days in Italy. They spent the rest of the time in France. How many days did they spend in France?

   A. 10   B. 9

   C. 5   D. 4

Word Problems #55

Directions: Write the > (greater than) or < (less than) symbol in the circle. Then answer the question.

1. Marvin has 659 tickets. Michelle has 337 tickets. Who has more tickets?

659 ◯ 337

_____ has more tickets.

2. Ellen has 120 cards. Edith has 562 cards. Who has more cards?

120 ◯ 562

_____ has more cards.

3. Peter caught 261 butterflies. Paula caught 892 butterflies. Who caught more butterflies?

261 ◯ 892

_____ caught more butterflies.

4. Sally counted 443 birds. Steven counted 434 birds. Who counted more birds?

443 ◯ 434

_____ counted more birds.

5. Ron found 516 pennies. Barb found 498 pennies. Who found more pennies?

516 ◯ 498

_____ found more pennies.

6. Mark made 429 baskets. Maria made 451 baskets. Who made more baskets?

429 ◯ 451

_____ made more baskets.

58

Word Problems #56

Directions: Read the clues. Write the student's house number in the box.

437   652   743   976

1.	**Roy's House**

- The numbers 3 and 7 are in his house address.

- His house has the lowest number.

Roy's house number ☐

2.	**Bob's House**

- Bob's house number has a 7 in it.

- Bob's house does not have the highest address on the street.

Bob's house number ☐

3.	**Sue's House**

- Sue's house does not have the highest number on the street.

- Sue's house has a 6 in the address.

Sue's house number ☐

4.	**Marie's House**

- Marie's house does not have a 3 as part of the address.

- Marie's house has a 7 in the tens place.

Marie's house number ☐

Word Problems #57

Directions: Read and study the house numbers and their patterns on First and Second Streets. Then read the riddles, study the clues, and write the answer.

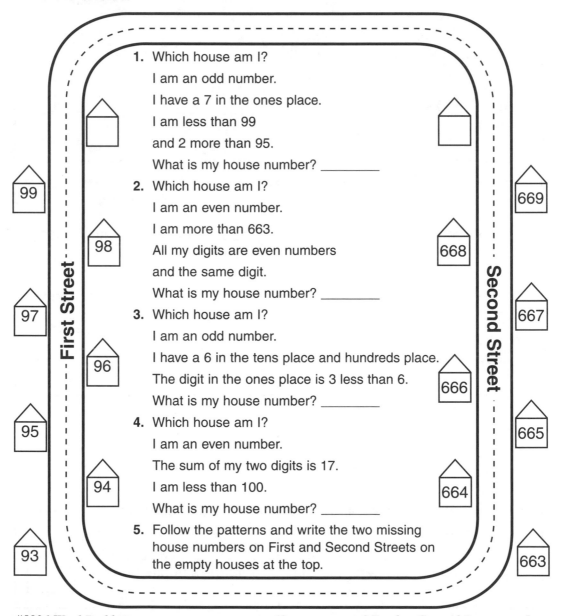

1. Which house am I?

   I am an odd number.

   I have a 7 in the ones place.

   I am less than 99

   and 2 more than 95.

   What is my house number? _____

2. Which house am I?

   I am an even number.

   I am more than 663.

   All my digits are even numbers

   and the same digit.

   What is my house number? _____

3. Which house am I?

   I am an odd number.

   I have a 6 in the tens place and hundreds place.

   The digit in the ones place is 3 less than 6.

   What is my house number? _____

4. Which house am I?

   I am an even number.

   The sum of my two digits is 17.

   I am less than 100.

   What is my house number? _____

5. Follow the patterns and write the two missing house numbers on First and Second Streets on the empty houses at the top.

First Street — 99, 98, 97, 96, 95, 94, 93

Second Street — 669, 668, 667, 666, 665, 664, 663

60

Answer Key

Page 4
1. 2
2. 4
3. 2
4. 9
5. 5
6. 3

Page 5
1. 9
2. 9
3. 6
4. 10
5. 3
6. 7

Page 6
1. 10, blue
2. 5, green
3. 8, blue
4. 9, green
5. 16, blue
6. 7, green
7. 14, blue
8. 11, green
9. 20, blue

Page 7
1. 7 − 6 = 1
2. 8 − 2 − 0 − 6 = 0
   or 8 − 8 = 0
3. 10 − 1 − 6 = 3
   or 10 − 7 = 3
4. 5 − 3 − 1 = 1 or
   5 − 4 = 1

Page 8
1. 3
2. 3
3. 8
4. 7

Page 9
1. 7; 10 − 3 = 7
2. 6; 20 − 14 = 6
3. 6; 12 − 6 = 6
4. 2; 5 − 3 = 2
5. 3; 12 − 9 = 3

Page 10
1. 14
2. 11
3. 6
4. 8
5. 9
6. 11

Page 11
1. D
2. D
3. A
4. C
5. C
6. B

Page 12
1. 14
2. 15
3. 6
4. 5
5. 17
6. 4

Page 13
1. 12 − 6 = 6
2. 11 + 5 = 16
3. 7 + 6 = 13
4. 10 + 8 = 18
5. 15 − 6 = 9
6. 16 − 3 = 13

Page 14
1. 14
2. 14
3. 6
4. 5

Page 15
1. 10
2. 14
3. 5
4. 9
5. 14
6. 6

Page 16
1. 8
2. 18
3. 7
4. 9
5. 6
6. 5

Page 17
1. 8
2. 10
3. 18
4. 6
5. 16
6. 15

Page 18
1. $14
2. 13
3. 9
4. 66

Page 19
1. 17
2. 15
3. 16
4. 14
5. 16

Page 20
1. 15
2. 14
3. 14
4. 13
5. 8
6. 12

Page 21
1. 15
2. 12
3. 5
4. 12
5. 16
6. 17
7. 8
8. 14

Page 22
1. 1 + 3 + 5 = 9
2. 8 + 10 + 1 = 19
3. 7 + 7 + 5 = 19
4. 3 + 2 + 5 = 10

Page 23
1. 10
2. 7
3. 11
4. 10
5. 8
6. 13

Page 24
1. 93
2. 79
3. 6
4. 7

Page 25
1. 90
2. 95
3. 35
4. 55
5. 55
6. 30

Page 26
1. 2
2. 33
3. 39
4. 10
5. 59
6. 55

Page 27
1. 79
2. 79
3. −
4. +
5. +
6. −

Page 28
1. 42
2. 69
3. 70
4. 10
5. 40
6. 39

Page 29
1. 32
2. 32
3. 300
4. 400

Page 30
1. 200
2. 300
3. 357
4. 635

Answer Key *(cont.)*

Page 31
1. 4 + 3 + 4 = 11
2. 12 + 8 + 16 = 36
3. 21 + 13 + 26 = 60
4. 19 + 5 + 31 = 55

Page 32
1. 93 − 68 = 25
2. 43 − 27 = 16
3. $53 − $28 = $25
4. $93 − $45 = $48

Page 33
1. 84   3. 90
2. 29   4. 44

Page 34
1. 42   4. 18
2. 19   5. 91
3. 48   6. 102

Page 35
1. 49   4. 37
2. 25   5. 76
3. 67   6. 88

Page 36
1. 84   4. 25
2. 71   5. 96
3. 22   6. 29

Page 37
1. 123 + 112 = 235
2. 312 + 200 = 512
3. 112 + 100 = 212
4. 134 + 234 = 368
5. 97 + 154 = 251

Page 38
1. D   3. B
2. C   4. D

Page 39
1. 87 − 73 = 14
2. 15 + 20 + 32 = 67
3. 87 + 15 = 102
4. 87 − 15 = 72

Page 40
1. 26   4. 24
2. 19   5. 19
3. 11

Page 41
1. 8   3. 21
2. 7   4. 12

Page 42
1. 6, 6
2. 8, 8
3. 24, 24
4. B

Page 43
1. 6, 6
2. 8, 8
3. 10, 10
4. 6, 6
5. 12, 12
6. 14, 14

Page 44
1. 2 x 1 = 2
2. 3 x 3 = 9
3. 5 x 8 = 40
4. 4 x 4 = 16
5. 5 x 3 = 15

Page 45
1. 20   4. 9
2. 12   5. 8
3. 10   6. 12

Page 46
1. C   3. D
2. C   4. D

Page 47
1. 59¢
2. 35¢
3. 30¢
4. 10¢
5. 15¢
6. 30¢

Page 48
1. 30¢, Yes
2. 36¢, No
3. 5
4. 25
5. 13¢
6. 81¢

Page 49
1. 25¢
2. 45¢
3. 12¢
4. 35¢
5. 75¢
6. 65¢

Page 50
1. $10.04
2. $28.13
3. $1.27
4. $8.29
5. $62.14

Page 51
1. C
2. 15
3. 35 ÷ 5 = 7
4. C

Page 52
1. 6:45
2. 11:30
3. 7:30 P.M.
4. 12:00 P.M.
5. 6:00 P.M.
6. 10:30 P.M.

Page 53
1. half past 8
2. a quarter till 4
3. half past 5
4. a quarter past 2
5. a quarter past 7
6. a quarter till 5

Page 54
1. 3   3. 3
2. 2   4. 4

Page 55
1. 13   4. 11
2. 15   5. 14
3. 16

Page 56
1. 409
2. 883
3. 291
4. 547
5. 622

Page 57
1. B   4. B
2. A   5. C
3. D

Page 58
1. >, Marvin
2. <, Edith
3. <, Paula
4. >, Sally
5. >, Ron
6. <, Maria

Page 59
1. 437   3. 652
2. 743   4. 976

Page 60
1. 97
2. 666
3. 663
4. 98
5. 100; 670

This Award
Is Presented To

_____

for

★ Doing Your Best

★ Trying Hard

★ Not Giving Up

★ Making a
  Great Effort